COLLECTION

ARTIFICIAL INTELLIGENCE

IMPACTS AND TRANSFORMATIONS

VOLUME 1

CHALLENGES AND SOLUTIONS IN DETECTING AI-GENERATED TEXTS

Prof. Marcão - Marcus Vinícius Pinto

Disclaimer:

Please note that the information contained in this document is for educational and entertainment purposes only. Every effort has been made to provide complete, accurate, up-to-date, and reliable information. No warranty of any kind is express or implied.

By reading this text, the reader agrees that under no circumstances are the authors liable for any losses, direct or indirect, incurred as a result of the use of the information contained in this book, including, but not limited to, errors, omissions, or inaccuracies.

ISBN: **9798344501949**

Publishing imprint: Independently published

Summary

Welcome.

We live in an era marked by profound transformations, where artificial intelligence (AI) redefines the limits of what is possible.

For professionals, academics, and tech enthusiasts, keeping up with these changes isn't just a matter of staying up-to-date — it's a matter of relevance in the job market and society as a whole.

With the growing volume of AI-generated texts, a new challenge arises: how to distinguish human authorship from artificial production? How to navigate in an environment where authorship becomes increasingly ambiguous?

It is precisely at this intersection of technology and human impact that this work "Impacts and Transformations - Volume 1: Challenges and Solutions in the Detection of Texts Generated by Artificial Intelligence" offers a rigorous but accessible exploration of a topic that affects several sectors.

This book has been carefully crafted to guide readers through the challenges of identifying AI-generated content and the broader implications of this technology in academia, journalism, and digital marketing, among others.

If you're an IT professional, a data expert, an educator, or even someone who works with content creation, this book was written with you in mind.

The reason is simple: AI-generated texts, such as those produced by ChatGPT and other generative models, are becoming increasingly common.

These tools offer enormous potential for automation, but they also present significant ethical and practical challenges, particularly with regard to the authenticity and reliability of information.

For educators and academics, the proliferation of AI-generated texts raises questions about academic integrity. How to distinguish the student's original work from a text generated by an algorithm? The second chapter of the book addresses exactly this point, exploring the existing solutions and limitations of current detection systems.

For journalists and media professionals, generative AI offers new opportunities, but it also puts pressure on the industry to adapt to a scenario where automated content can compete with human production in terms of volume and speed. This book examines how AI detection tools can be applied to preserve the quality and veracity of information.

In the field of digital marketing, where content creation is the heart of the strategy, professionals will find valuable insights on how to utilize these technologies without compromising the authenticity of their brand. The book not only looks at the advantages of these tools, but also exposes the limitations and challenges that professionals will face when incorporating AI into their strategies.

This book is not restricted to listing problems; It offers practical and reasoned solutions. The comparative analysis of AI detectors, covered in chapters five and six, provides a practical guide to choosing the most appropriate tools for each context.

Each detector is examined in depth, with a technical analysis that includes its characteristics, advantages, and limitations. This technical content is balanced by reflections on the ethical and social implications, providing the reader with a holistic view of the field.

One of the most thought-provoking aspects of this volume is the case study on ChatGPT, one of the most popular and influential generative AI models of the moment.

Throughout the ninth chapter, we explore the unique challenges this model brings to detection systems and the emerging strategies that seek to address these obstacles.

This analysis not only reveals the technical complexities involved, but also the social and ethical consequences of living with machines that are increasingly adept at producing content that mimics human authorship.

"Impacts and Transformations - Volume 1" also stands out for looking beyond the current scenario. The last chapter invites the reader to reflect on the future of coexistence between humans and generative AI, offering a provocative look at how society can and should shape this ever-evolving relationship.

If you're a professional looking for tools to navigate the growing volume of AI-generated content, or if you're an academic who cares about the ethical and technical issues that this phenomenon brings, this book is for you.

Through a rigorous yet accessible approach, he offers the knowledge needed to meet the challenges of an era where authorship is no longer just a matter of who writes, but of how we understand what is "written."

I invite you to embark on this reading, which is both a critical analysis and a practical guide to the transformative impact of artificial intelligence on our relationship with writing, knowledge, and truth.

This volume is part of the collection "Artificial Intelligence: The Power of Data", which explores the impacts and transformations that AI can bring to different areas of activity.

Together, the books in the collection offer a complete picture, helping professionals understand how this technological revolution can optimize data governance, improve processes, and promote effective leadership.

However, this is just the beginning of an essential journey in the field of artificial intelligence. By purchasing and reading the other volumes of the collection, you will gain a holistic and deep insight into how AI can be a transformative force in your operations and leadership, creating a more efficient, inclusive, and innovative future for your organization.

Happy reading!
Good learning!

Prof. Marcão - Marcus Vinícius Pinto

M. Sc. in Information Technology
Specialist in Information Technology.
Consultant, Mentor and Speaker on Artificial Intelligence,
Information Architecture and Data Governance.
Founder, CEO, teacher and
pedagogical advisor at MVP Consult.

1 The era of ambiguous authorship: challenges and solutions in the detection of texts generated by artificial intelligence.

"What we call the Information Revolution
in fact, it is a Knowledge Revolution"
Peter Drucker

At the dawn of the twenty-first century, we are witnessing a quiet revolution that is redefining the paradigms of textual creation and authorship.

Artificial intelligence (AI), once confined to the realms of science fiction and research labs, has emerged as a transformative force in content production, challenging our traditional conceptions of creativity, originality, and even the very nature of human expression.

This phenomenon, catalyzed by the advent of generative AI systems such as ChatGPT, developed by OpenAI, ushers in an era of "ambiguous authorship," where the line between human creation and machinic generation becomes increasingly blurred and blurred.

The rise of generative AIs, capable of producing texts that emulate with remarkable precision the style and complexity of human writing, raises profound questions that transcend the technical and academic spheres, entering the domains of ethics, intellectual property, and epistemology itself.

How to distinguish, in a world saturated with information, the authentic voice of the human author from the synthetic eloquence of an algorithm? What are the implications of this revolution for education, journalism, literature and other fundamental areas of cultural and intellectual production?

In this context of uncertainty and transformation, a new category of technological tools is emerging AI detectors. These instruments, conceived as gatekeepers of authenticity in the digital age, promise to offer a means of navigating the uncertain terrain of contemporary authorship. However, its very existence raises additional questions about privacy, reliability, and the ethical limits of automated textual analysis.

This treatise proposes to explore, with depth and academic rigor, the complex and changing landscape of AI-generated text detection.

We will examine not only the technologies and methodologies employed in this new frontier of textual analysis, but also their broader implications for society, culture, and human knowledge.

Through a detailed analysis of specific tools, case studies, and theoretical perspectives, we will seek to illuminate the challenges and opportunities that present themselves at this crucial intersection between human and artificial intelligence.

2 The advent of Generative AI and its impact on textual production.

2.1 Historical evolution of AI in text generation.

The journey of artificial intelligence in text generation dates back to the first decades of computing. In the 1950s, Alan Turing proposed the famous "Turing Test," a conceptual framework that laid the groundwork for evaluating a machine's ability to exhibit intelligent behavior indistinguishable from humans.

This test, although originally conceived as a thought experiment, has become a guiding paradigm in the development of conversational and generative AI systems.

In the 1960s, Joseph Weizenbaum developed ELIZA, one of the first natural language processing programs capable of simulating conversation. Although ELIZA operated on simple recognition and substitution patterns, its impact was profound, demonstrating the potential and limitations of early approaches to machine text generation.

Subsequent decades witnessed incremental advances, with the development of rules-based systems and, later, statistics.

However, it was the emergence of deep neural networks, and in particular transformer-based language models, that revolutionized the field of AI text generation.

2.2 The emergence of ChatGPT and its revolution.

OpenAI's launch of ChatGPT in 2022 marked a turning point in the history of generative AI.

Based on the GPT (Generative Pre-trained Transformer) architecture, ChatGPT has demonstrated an unprecedented ability to generate coherent, contextually relevant, and stylistically diverse text.

His ability to understand and respond to a wide range of prompts, from casual conversations to complex analysis, has captured the imagination of audiences and professionals in a variety of fields.

ChatGPT's impact transcends its impressive technical performance. It catalyzed a paradigm shift in the public perception of AI by making the potential of artificial intelligence tangible and accessible to millions of users around the world.

This democratization of access to generative AI has profound implications for diverse sectors, from education and journalism to literary creation and academic research.

2.3   Ethical and social implications.

The rise of systems like ChatGPT raises complex ethical and social questions. The ease with which these systems can generate high-quality content raises concerns about:

- Authenticity and originality: How do we define authorship in an era where machines can produce texts indistinguishable from humans?

- Misinformation and Fake News: The potential of using AI to generate misleading content on a large scale poses a significant threat to information integrity.

- Impact on the job market: Writing automation can have profound implications for professionals in a variety of fields, from journalists to advertising copywriters.

- Biases and biases: AI models, trained on vast corpuses of human text, can perpetuate and amplify existing biases.

Scholars such as Luciano Floridi of the University of Oxford argue that we are entering an era of "infosphere," where the distinction between the real and the artificial becomes increasingly blurred.

In this context, the ability to discern between human-generated and AI-generated content becomes not just a technical issue, but an ethical and social imperative.

3   Technical Fundamentals of AI Detection.

3.1   Principles of computational linguistic analysis.

The detection of AI-generated texts is based on advanced principles of computational linguistic analysis. This discipline, which intersects linguistics, computer science, and artificial intelligence, seeks to develop methods and algorithms to analyze and understand human language in its written and spoken forms.

Noam Chomsky, a pioneering linguist, laid the theoretical foundation for understanding the deep structure of language, significantly influencing the field of computational linguistics.

His theories on generative grammar and deep syntactic structures provided a conceptual framework for the automated analysis of language.

In the detection of AI-generated texts, several approaches to computational linguistic analysis are employed:

1   Syntactic analysis: examines the grammatical structure of sentences, identifying patterns that may be characteristic of AI-generated text.

2   Semantic analysis: investigates the meaning and coherence of the text, looking for inconsistencies or semantic patterns typical of AI.

3   Stylometric analysis: studies stylistic characteristics of the text, such as word choice, sentence length, and lexical variability.

4   Cohesion and coherence analysis evaluates how ideas are connected and whether the flow of the text is natural and logical.

3.2   Machine learning algorithms and techniques.

Modern AI detectors employ a variety of machine learning algorithms to discern between human and AI-generated texts:

1 Recurrent neural networks (RNNs): particularly effective at analyzing text sequences, picking up long-term dependencies.

2 Transformers: architecture that revolutionized natural language processing, being the basis of models such as BERT and GPT.

3 Statistical language models: analyze the probability of word sequences, identifying unusual patterns.

4 Text classifiers: Algorithms such as SVM (Support Vector Machines) and Random Forests are trained on large corpuses of labeled texts to distinguish between human and artificial authorship.

5 Entropy analysis: measures the predictability and randomness of text, since AI-generated texts can exhibit different entropy patterns than humans.

The work of researchers such as Yoshua Bengio, Geoffrey Hinton, and Yann LeCun, pioneers in deep learning, has been instrumental in the development of these advanced textual analysis techniques.

3.3   Technical challenges in detection.

AI-generated text detection faces several technical challenges:

1 Rapid evolution of AI models: As generative models become more sophisticated, detectors constantly need to adapt.

2 Linguistic variability: The diversity of styles, genres, and languages makes it difficult to create a universally effective detector.

3   False positives and negatives: Balancing detector sensitivity to minimize misclassification is an ongoing challenge.

4   Hybrid texts: Content that combines human authorship and AI is particularly difficult to classify.

5   Evasion techniques: Methods for "humanizing" AI-generated text are constantly developing, challenging detectors.

Researchers such as Dario Amodei of OpenAI and Emily M. Bender of the University of Washington have contributed significantly to the understanding of these challenges and the development of robust solutions.

4   Comparative analysis of AI detectors.

4.1   Smodin.

Smodin represents a multifaceted approach to AI-generated content detection, especially effective for Portuguese texts. Its methodology is based on a combination of natural language processing (NLP) and machine learning techniques.

4.1.1   Technical Characteristics.

- Uses pre-trained language models adapted specifically for Portuguese.

- Employs advanced stylometric analysis to identify linguistic nuances typical of AI.

- Integrates a scoring system that indicates the probability of authorship by AI.

4.1.2   Advantages.

- High accuracy in detecting texts in Portuguese.

- Intuitive and easy-to-use interface.

- Offers additional features like rewriting and summarization.

4.1.3   Limitations.

- The character limit in the free version may be restrictive for more extensive analysis.

- Effectiveness may vary depending on the complexity and style of the text being analyzed.

4.2   isgen.ai.

isgen.ai stands out for its multilingual approach to AI detection utilizing cutting-edge technologies in NLP.

4.2.1   Technical characteristics.

- Employs transformers language models adapted for multiple languages.

- Uses deep semantic analysis techniques to identify subtle AI generation patterns.

- Incorporates a continuous learning system that adapts to new AI writing patterns.

4.2.2   Advantages.

- Detection capacity in several languages.

- Advanced identification system in paid plans.

- High monthly processing capacity.

4.2.3   Limitations.

- Accuracy may vary between different languages.

- The basic identification system in the free version may be less robust.

4.3   ZeroGPT.

ZeroGPT, while initially focused on Portuguese from Portugal, offers an interesting approach to AI detection that may be applicable to Brazilian Portuguese.

4.3.1   Technical characteristics.

- Uses textual cohesion analysis to identify inconsistencies typical of AI-generated text.

- Employs data visualization techniques to highlight suspicious areas in the text.

- Integrates narrative flow analysis to detect unnatural patterns of textual progression.

4.3.2   Advantages.

- Visual highlighting of potentially AI-generated snippets.

- Intuitive and easy-to-interpret interface.

- Potential for adaptation to close linguistic variants.

4.3.3   Limitations.

- Lower accuracy for Brazilian Portuguese texts compared to Portuguese from Portugal.

- Relatively low character limit in the free version.

4.4   detecting-ai.com.

Detecting-ai.com takes a balanced approach between accessibility and advanced functionality.

4.4.1   Technical characteristics.

- Utilizes a combination of statistical analysis and deep learning models.

- Employs textual entropy analysis techniques to identify non-human patterns.

- Integrates a user feedback system to continuously improve accuracy.

4.4.2   Advantages.

- Good balance between functionality and price.

- Special options for educational institutions.

- Robust detection system in paid plans.

4.4.3   Limitations.

- The daily detection limit in the free version may be restrictive for frequent users.

- Effectiveness may vary depending on the type and length of the text analyzed.

4.5   undetectable.ai

Undetectable.ai distinguishes itself by offering not only detection but also "humanization" of AI-generated text.

4.5.1   Technical characteristics.

- Employs advanced GPT-based text generation and modification techniques.

- Utilizes style and tone analysis to identify and adjust typical AI characteristics.

- Integrates a human review system to calibrate and validate results.

4.5.2   Advantages.

- Unique ability to "humanize" AI-generated text.

- Flexibility in pricing plans based on the volume of usage.

- Potential for use in ethical AI research and development.

4.5.3   Limitations.

- The "humanization" functionality raises ethical questions about authenticity.

- It can be more complex to use compared to pure detectors.

- Potential for misuse in the creation of misleading content.

5   Comparative analysis.

When comparing these tools, we observe a diversity of approaches and focuses. Smodin and isgen.ai excel at multilingual detection, with Smodin offering a specific advantage for Portuguese.

ZeroGPT brings an interesting visual approach, albeit with linguistic limitations. Detecting-ai.com offers a good balance between functionality and affordability, making it an attractive option for users with varying needs.

Undetectable.ai, in turn, presents a unique proposal with its text "humanization" functionality, although this raises important ethical questions.

Each tool has its strengths and weaknesses, adapting to different needs and contexts:

1   Smodin is particularly effective for users who work primarily with texts in Portuguese, offering high accuracy in this language. Its intuitive interface and additional rewriting and summarizing functionalities make it a versatile choice for content professionals and educators alike.

2   isgen.ai stands out for its robust multilingual approach, making it ideal for international organizations or researchers dealing with texts in multiple languages. Its advanced identification system in paid plans offers a deeper and more detailed analysis.

3   ZeroGPT, despite its limitations with Brazilian Portuguese, offers a unique visual approach that can be particularly useful for detailed analysis of long texts. Its ability to visually highlight suspicious excerpts can be valuable to editors and reviewers.

4   Detecting-ai.com presents a balanced solution, with affordable options for both casual users and educational institutions. Its

integration of user feedback to continuously improve accuracy is a key differentiator.

5   Undetectable.ai stands out for its dual approach to detection and "humanization". This unique feature makes it an interesting tool for researchers studying the interaction between human and AI-generated text, although it also raises ethical concerns about the authenticity of the content.

When choosing between these tools, users should consider not only the technical effectiveness, but also their specific needs, budget, and the ethical implications of using these technologies.

For users focused on content in Portuguese, Smodin may be the most suitable choice. For organizations that deal with multiple languages, isgen.ai offers a more comprehensive solution.

ZeroGPT can be ideal for those who value visual analysis, while Detecting-ai.com offers a more balanced solution for users with diverse needs.

It is important to note that as generative AI models continue to evolve rapidly, these detection tools will also need to constantly adapt.

Users should be on the lookout for continuous updates and improvements to these platforms to ensure they remain effective against the latest AI text generation technologies.

Additionally, it is crucial to consider the broader context in which these tools are used. They should not be seen as definitive solutions, but as part of a broader set of practices to ensure the integrity and authenticity of content.

Education on the ethical use of AI, clear policies in academic institutions and organizations, and an ongoing dialogue about the implications of generative AI are equally important.

Ultimately, choosing the most appropriate AI detection tool will depend on a combination of technical, practical, and ethical factors, reflecting the specific needs and values of the user or organization.

6 Implications and practical applications of AI detectors.

6.1   Impact on the academic environment.

The proliferation of AI-generated texts has sparked a revolution in academia, challenging traditional conceptions of authorship, academic integrity, and knowledge assessment. AI detectors emerge as crucial tools in this new educational paradigm.

Dr. Sarah Eaton of the University of Calgary, an expert in academic integrity, argues that introducing generative AI technologies into the educational environment not only represents a challenge, but also an opportunity to rethink teaching and assessment methods.

She proposes that educational institutions should adapt their policies and practices to incorporate the ethical use of AI, rather than simply banning it.

Practical Applications:

1. Plagiarism prevention: AI detectors can be integrated into existing plagiarism checker systems, amplifying their effectiveness.

2. Evaluation of works: teachers can use these tools to identify submissions potentially generated by AI, promoting discussions about authorship and originality.

3. Development of critical skills: The use of detectors can encourage students to develop critical thinking and information synthesis skills, as opposed to merely reproducing content.

6.2   Implications for journalism and media.

In the journalistic field, the ability to generate text quickly and at scale through AI presents both significant opportunities and challenges.

Nicholas Diakopoulos, a professor of Communication at Northwestern University and an expert in computational journalism, points out that AI has the potential to increase journalistic productivity, but it also raises questions about the authenticity and reliability of news.

Practical Applications:

1. Source verification: AI detectors can be used to verify the authenticity of press releases and other sources of information.

2. Combating disinformation: these tools can help identify fake news generated en masse by AI systems.

3. Editorial transparency: newspapers and news portals can use detectors to guarantee and demonstrate human authorship of their content.

6.3   Impact on the content and digital marketing industry.

The digital marketing and content industry are experiencing a radical transformation with the introduction of generative AI tools.

Ann Handley, a bestselling author and content marketing expert, argues that AI will not replace human content creators, but will fundamentally change the nature of their work, focusing more on strategy, creativity, and oversight.

Practical Applications:

1. Brand authenticity: Companies can use detectors to ensure that their content maintains an authentic and human voice.

2. Competitive analysis: Marketers can analyze competitors' content to identify the use of AI in content production.

3. Compliance and transparency: In regulated industries, detectors can help ensure that the content generated complies with disclosure guidelines.

4.4 Legal and Ethical Considerations

The use of AI detectors raises complex legal and ethical issues. Lawrence Lessig, a Harvard law professor and a pioneer in cyber law, argues that the advancement of generative AI requires a fundamental overhaul of our intellectual property and copyright laws.

Key issues:

1. Privacy: The use of AI detectors on a large scale can raise concerns about surveillance and invasion of privacy.

2. Algorithmic discrimination: There is a risk that AI detectors could exhibit biases, potentially discriminating against certain writing styles or language groups.

3. Legal liability: Who is responsible for misclassification that could result in reputational or financial damage?

7   Future of AI sensing and human-machine coexistence

As generative AI models continue to evolve, it is likely that we will see an arms race between AI generators and detectors.

Yoshua Bengio, a pioneer in deep learning and a professor at the University of Montreal, predicts that we will eventually reach a point where distinguishing between human-generated and AI-generated content will become virtually impossible.

Future Trends:

1. Multimodal detection: Future detectors will be able to analyze not only text, but also AI-generated images, audio, and video.

2. Blockchain integration: Distributed ledger technologies can be used to create an immutable history of authorship and content changes.

3. Augmented authorship assistants: instead of simply detecting, future tools will be able to work in symbiosis with human authors, suggesting improvements and verifying originality in real time.

8   Case study – ChatGPT and its impact on AI detection.

8.1   The ChatGPT phenomenon.

OpenAI's launch of ChatGPT in November 2022 marked a turning point in the history of generative AI. This language model, based on the Generative Pre-trained Transformer (GPT) architecture, has demonstrated an unprecedented ability to generate coherent, contextually relevant, and stylistically diverse text in response to a wide range of prompts.

Distinctive Features of ChatGPT:

1. Advanced contextualization: ability to maintain coherence throughout extensive conversations.

2. Versatility: ability to address diverse topics, from technical analysis to literary creation.

3. Small-sample learning: Ability to adapt quickly to new types of tasks with minimal instruction.

8.2   Unique Challenges in ChatGPT Text Detection.

ChatGPT's sophistication presents significant challenges for existing AI detectors:

1. Stylistic Variability: ChatGPT can emulate various writing styles, making it difficult to identify consistent patterns.

2. Deep Contextualization: Its ability to maintain context throughout long texts makes it more difficult to detect it based on coherence analysis.

3. Adaptability: The model can adjust its output based on specific instructions, potentially evading known detection techniques.

Dario Amodei, chief scientist at Anthropic and former researcher at OpenAI, points out that "ChatGPT represents a qualitative leap in text generation, making the distinction between human and artificial content increasingly subtle."

8.3 Emerging strategies for detecting ChatGPT texts.

In response to the challenges presented by ChatGPT, researchers and developers are exploring new approaches:

1. Analysis of Patterns of Reasoning: examining not only the final text, but the logical structure and underlying patterns of reasoning.

2. Detection of subtle inconsistencies: focusing on small inconsistencies or "slips" that can occur in long AI-generated texts.

3. Broad context analysis: considering the broader context in which the text was produced, including metadata and circumstantial information.

8.4 Ethical and Social Implications of ChatGPT.

The advent of ChatGPT has intensified ethical and social debates about the use of generative AI:

1. Large-scale disinformation: The ease of generating compelling content raises concerns about the proliferation of fake news and propaganda.

2. Impact on employment: questions about the future of professions based on writing and content creation.

3. Intellectual property: debates about authorship and copyright of content generated or co-created with AI.

Luciano Floridi, professor of Philosophy and Ethics of Information at the University of Oxford, argues that "ChatGPT is not just a tool, but an agent that is reshaping our understanding of creativity and authorship."

9 The future of coexistence between humans and generative AI

As models like ChatGPT become more integrated into our social and professional fabric, the question is no longer simply how to detect them, but how to coexist and collaborate with them in an ethical and productive way.

Trends and Forecasts:

1. Augmented AI vs. autonomous AI: Move toward systems that augment human capability rather than replace it altogether.

2. Adaptive education: educational systems that incorporate generative AI as a tool for learning and creation.

3. New forms of creativity: emergence of forms of art and expression that fuse human and artificial creativity.

Stuart Russell, professor of Computer Science at UC Berkeley and author of "Human Compatible: Artificial Intelligence and the Problem of Control," emphasizes the need to develop AI that aligns with human values: "The challenge is not just to create more powerful AI, but to ensure that it benefits humanity as a whole."

10 Conclusion.

The rise of AI detectors, especially in the context of the emergence of advanced models like ChatGPT, marks a new frontier in the interface between technology and society.

These tools are not just technical tools, but catalysts for profound changes in how we conceive of authorship, authenticity, and creativity.

As we move forward in this new era, it is crucial to maintain a balance between technological innovation and ethical considerations. AI detection should not be seen as a definitive solution, but as part of a broader ecosystem of practices and policies that promote transparency, integrity, and responsible use of technology.

The future is likely to see an ever-deeper integration between human and artificial creativity, challenging our traditional notions of authorship and originality.

In this context, education, regulation, and ongoing dialogue between technologists, ethicists, and policymakers will be essential to navigate the challenges and opportunities that present themselves.

Ultimately, the goal is not to create an insurmountable divide between humans and machine, but to foster an environment where both can coexist and collaborate in ways that amplify human potential and promote social well-being.

AI detectors, in this scenario, are not just tools of distinction, but instruments that help us actively navigate and shape our evolving relationship with artificial intelligence.

In this volume, "Impacts and Transformations - Volume 1: Challenges and Solutions in AI-Generated Text Detection," we take a deep dive into the complexities that artificial intelligence (AI) introduces in the field of text generation and detection.

Throughout this book, we seek not only to identify the problems, but also to offer practical and reasonable solutions, guided by ethical principles and technological innovations.

Our goal was to provide a comprehensive understanding of the challenges and opportunities that AI presents in text generation and detection, empowering readers to navigate this ever-evolving field in an informed and critical manner.

However, this is just one step in an essential journey in the field of artificial intelligence. This volume is part of a larger collection, "Artificial Intelligence: The Power of Data," which explores, in depth, different aspects of AI and data science.

The other volumes address equally crucial topics, such as the integration of AI systems, predictive analytics, and the use of advanced algorithms for decision-making.

By purchasing and reading the other books in the collection, you will have a holistic and deep view that will allow you not only to optimize data governance, but also to enhance the impact of artificial intelligence on your operations.

Each book complements the previous one by offering a detailed and expert understanding of essential components of AI, from technical infrastructure to practical applications in various industries.

This collection is an indispensable tool for professionals, researchers, and enthusiasts who want to master the multiple facets of artificial intelligence and apply this knowledge strategically and effectively in their respective fields of expertise.

I invite you to continue this journey by exploring the other volumes of "Artificial Intelligence: The Power of Data".

Discover how each component covered enriches your understanding and empowers you to meet the challenges and seize the opportunities that AI offers.

Get ready to transform your understanding and apply artificial intelligence in innovative and impactful ways in your career and your organization.

11 Bibliography.

B. SETTLES, Active learning literature survey, Technical Report, University of Wisconsin-Madison D partment of Computer Sciences, 2009.

BERKOVSKY, K. Yu, S. CONWAY, D. TAIB, R., ZHOU, J. and CHEN, F. (2018). Do I trust a machine? Differences in user trust based on system performance, in: Human and Machine Learning, Springer, pp. 245–264.

BERNERS-Lee, T., MANSOUR, E., SAMBRA, A., et al. (2016). A Demonstration of the Solid Platform for Social Web Applications. Published inThe Web Conference. Available at https://dl.acm.org/doi/10.1145/2872518.2890529.

BRETON, Philippe & PROULX, Serge (1989). L'explosion de la communication. La naissance d'une nouvelle idéologie. Paris: La Découverte.

BROWN, C. (2018). Utilizing NoSQL Databases and Big Data Frameworks in AI Projects. Big Data Symposium Proceedings.

CHEN, M., WEI, Z., HUANG, Z., DING, B., & LI, Y. (2020) Simple and deep graph convolutional networks. In ICML.

CRAWFORD, K. Ethics and Transparency in Artificial Intelligence. Research in AI Ethics, 2021.

Data Management Association International (DAMA). (2020). "Data Governance Best Practices for NoSQL Databases and Graphs". DAMA White Paper Series, 7.

DAVENPORT, T. Organizational Culture and Data Governance. Harvard Business Review, 2017.

DAVENPORT, T.H. (2018). The Essential Role of Data Security in Data Governance. Harvard Business Review.

DAVENPORT, T.H., & DYCHE, J. (2013). Big Data in Big Companies. Harvard Business Review, 91(6), 60-68.

FU, Y., PENG, H., SABHARWAL, A., CLARK, P., & KHOT, T. (2022). Complexity-based prompting for multi-step reasoning. arXiv preprint arXiv:2210.00720.

FU, Z., XIANG, T., KODIROV, E., & GONG, S. (2017). Zero-shot learning on semantic class prototype graph. IEEE Transactions on Pattern Analysis and Machine Intelligence, 40(8), 2009–2022.

GEVA, M., KHASHABI, D., SEGAL, E., KHOT, T., ROTH, D., & BERANT, J. (2021). Did Aristotle use a laptop? A question answering benchmark with implicit reasoning strategies. Transactions of the Association for Computational Linguistics, 9, 346–361.

GLIWA, B., MOCHOL, I., BIESEK, M., & WAWER, A. (2019). Samsum corpus: A human-annotated dialogue dataset for abstractive summarization. arXiv preprint arXiv:1911.12237.

GOERTZEL, B. (2014). Artificial general intelligence: concept, state of the art, and future prospects. Journal of Artificial General Intelligence, 5(1), 1.

GUO, B., Zhang, X., WANG, Z., Jiang, M., NIE, J., DING, Y., YUE, J., & Wu, Y. (2023). How close is ChatGPT to human experts? Comparison corpus, evaluation, and detection. ar Xiv preprint arXiv:2301.07597.

HAWKINS, J., & BLAKESLEE, S. (2004). On Intelligence. New York: Times Books.

HELBING, D. (2014). The World after Big Data: What the Digital Revolution Means for Us. Available at: http://papers.ssrn.com/sol3/papers.cfm?abstract_id=2438957.

IMHOFF, C. (2020). Holistic Approach to Data Governance for AI. Boulder BI Brain Trust.

JAJODIA, S., SAMARATI, P., & SUBRAHMANIAN, V. S. (2008). Handbook of Database Security: JAPEC, L., KREUTER, F., BERG, M., BIEMER, P., DECKER, P., LAMPE, C., ... & USHER, A. (2015). Big Data in Survey Research: AAPOR Task Force Report. Public Opinion Quarterly, 79(4), 839-880.

JOHNSON, M. (2018). Data Quality: A Key Factor in Machine.

JONES, A. et al. (2018). "Implementing Data Governance in a NoSQL Graph Database Environment". Proceedings of the International Conference on Data Management, 132-145.

LACITY, M. (2019). Data Governance for AI: Why it's Necessary for Success. Forbes.

LADLEY, J. (2019). Data Governance: How to Design, Deploy, and Sustain an Effective Data Governance Program. Oxford, UK: Elsevier.

LOGAN, D. (2020). The Emergence of the Chief Data Officer. Journal of Data Management, 20(2), 47-52.

LUCKER, J. Data Governance in the Age of Artificial Intelligence. Deloitte, 2019.

OTTO, B., & WEBER, Kristin. (2013). Data governance. In Business & Information Systems Engineering.

REDMAN, R T.C. (2008). Data Governance. Bridgewater, NJ: Technics Publications.

REDMAN, T.C. & SOARES, D. D. (2021). Application of AI in Data Governance. AI Magazine, 37(4), 78-85.

RUSSELL, S., & NORVIG, P. (2009). "Artificial Intelligence: A Modern Approach".

S.A. CAMBO and D. GERGLE, User-Centred Evaluation for Machine Learning, in: Human and Machine

SHIH, P.C. (2018) Beyond Human-in-the-Loop: Empowering End-Users with Transparent Machine Learning, in: Human and Machine Learning, Springer, 2018, pp. 37–54.

SHMUELI, G., & KOPPIUS, O.R. (2011). Predictive Analytics in Information Systems Research. Management Information Systems Quarterly, 35(3), 553-572.

SOARES, S. (2012). Data Governance Tools: Evaluation Criteria, Big Data Governance, and Alignment with Enterprise Data Management. MC Press.

SOARES, S. (2013). Big Data Governance: An Emerging Imperative. MC Press.

TURING, A. (1950). "Computing Machinery and Intelligence". IN: Mind, Volume 59, Number 236, pp. 433-460. Edinburgh: Thomas Nelson & Sons.

WELLS, A., & CHIANG, K. (2016). Data-Driven Leadership. Wiley.

WIECZOREK, M., & MERTENS, P. (2019). Data Governance: A Practical Guide. Englewood Cliffs, NJ: Prentice Hall.

ZHENG, R. and GREENBERG, K. (2018). Effective Design in Human and Machine Learning: A Cognitive Perspective, in: Human and Machine Learning, Springer, pp. 55–74.

12 Discover the Complete Collection "Artificial Intelligence and the Power of Data" – An Invitation to Transform Your Career and Knowledge.

The "Artificial Intelligence and the Power of Data" Collection was created for those who want not only to understand Artificial Intelligence (AI), but also to apply it strategically and practically.

In a series of carefully crafted volumes, I unravel complex concepts in a clear and accessible manner, ensuring the reader has a thorough understanding of AI and its impact on modern societies.

No matter what level of familiarity with the topic, this collection turns the difficult into the didactic, theoretical into the applicable, and the technical into something powerful for your career.

12.1   Why buy this collection?

We are living through an unprecedented technological revolution, where AI is the driving force in areas such as medicine, finance, education, government, and entertainment.

The collection "Artificial Intelligence and the Power of Data" dives deep into all these sectors, with practical examples and reflections that go far beyond traditional concepts.

You'll find both the technical expertise and the ethical and social implications of AI encouraging you to see this technology not just as a tool, but as a true agent of transformation.

Each volume is a fundamental piece of this innovative puzzle: from machine learning to data governance and from ethics to practical application.

With the guidance of an experienced author who combines academic research with years of hands-on practice, this collection is more than a set of books – it's an indispensable guide for anyone looking to navigate and excel in this burgeoning field.

12.2   Target Audience of this Collection?

This collection is for everyone who wants to play a prominent role in the age of AI:

- ✓ Tech Professionals: Receive deep technical insights to expand their skills.

- ✓ Students and the Curious: have access to clear explanations that facilitate the understanding of the complex universe of AI.

- ✓ Managers, business leaders, and policymakers will also benefit from the strategic vision on AI, which is essential for making well-informed decisions.

- ✓ Professionals in Career Transition: Professionals in career transition or interested in specializing in AI will find here complete material to build their learning trajectory.

12.3   Much More Than Technique – A Complete Transformation.

This collection is not just a series of technical books; It is a tool for intellectual and professional growth.

With it, you go far beyond theory: each volume invites you to a deep reflection on the future of humanity in a world where machines and algorithms are increasingly present.

This is your invitation to master the knowledge that will define the future and become part of the transformation that Artificial Intelligence brings to the world.

Be a leader in your industry, master the skills the market demands, and prepare for the future with the "Artificial Intelligence and the Power of Data" collection.

This is not just a purchase; It is a decisive investment in your learning and professional development journey.

Prof. Marcão - Marcus Vinícius Pinto

M. Sc. in Information Technology.
Specialist in Artificial Intelligence, Data
Governance and Information Architecture.

13 The Books of the Collection.

13.1   Data, Information and Knowledge in the era of Artificial Intelligence.

This book essentially explores the theoretical and practical foundations of Artificial Intelligence, from data collection to its transformation into intelligence. It focuses primarily on machine learning, AI training, and neural networks.

13.2   From Data to Gold: How to Turn Information into Wisdom in the Age of AI.

This book offers critical analysis on the evolution of Artificial Intelligence, from raw data to the creation of artificial wisdom, integrating neural networks, deep learning, and knowledge modeling.

It presents practical examples in health, finance, and education, and addresses ethical and technical challenges.

13.3   Challenges and Limitations of Data in AI.

The book offers an in-depth analysis of the role of data in the development of AI exploring topics such as quality, bias, privacy, security, and scalability with practical case studies in healthcare, finance, and public safety.

13.4   Historical Data in Databases for AI: Structures, Preservation, and Purge.

This book investigates how historical data management is essential to the success of AI projects. It addresses the relevance of ISO standards to ensure quality and safety, in addition to analyzing trends and innovations in data processing.

13.5   Controlled Vocabulary for Data Dictionary: A Complete Guide.

This comprehensive guide explores the advantages and challenges of implementing controlled vocabularies in the context of AI and information science. With a detailed approach, it covers everything from the naming of data elements to the interactions between semantics and cognition.

13.6   Data Curation and Management for the Age of AI.

This book presents advanced strategies for transforming raw data into valuable insights, with a focus on meticulous curation and efficient data management. In addition to technical solutions, it addresses ethical and legal issues, empowering the reader to face the complex challenges of information.

13.7   Information Architecture.

The book addresses data management in the digital age, combining theory and practice to create efficient and scalable AI systems, with insights into modeling and ethical and legal challenges.

13.8   Fundamentals: The Essentials of Mastering Artificial Intelligence.

An essential work for anyone who wants to master the key concepts of AI, with an accessible approach and practical examples. The book explores innovations such as Machine Learning and Natural Language Processing, as well as ethical and legal challenges, and offers a clear view of the impact of AI on various industries.

13.9   LLMS - Large-Scale Language Models.

This essential guide helps you understand the revolution of Large-Scale Language Models (LLMs) in AI.

The book explores the evolution of GPTs and the latest innovations in human-computer interaction, offering practical insights into their impact on industries such as healthcare, education, and finance.

13.10   Machine Learning: Fundamentals and Advances.

This book offers a comprehensive overview of supervised and unsupervised algorithms, deep neural networks, and federated learning. In addition to addressing issues of ethics and explainability of models.

13.11   Inside Synthetic Minds.

This book reveals how these 'synthetic minds' are redefining creativity, work, and human interactions. This work presents a detailed analysis of the challenges and opportunities provided by these technologies, exploring their profound impact on society.

13.12   The Issue of Copyright.

This book invites the reader to explore the future of creativity in a world where human-machine collaboration is a reality, addressing questions about authorship, originality, and intellectual property in the age of generative AIs.

13.13   1121 Questions and Answers: From Basic to Complex – Part 1 to 4.

Organized into four volumes, these questions serve as essential practical guides to mastering key AI concepts.

Part 1 addresses information, data, geoprocessing, the evolution of artificial intelligence, its historical milestones and basic concepts.

Part 2 delves into complex concepts such as machine learning, natural language processing, computer vision, robotics, and decision algorithms.

Part 3 addresses issues such as data privacy, work automation, and the impact of large-scale language models (LLMs).

Part 4 explores the central role of data in the age of artificial intelligence, delving into the fundamentals of AI and its applications in areas such as mental health, government, and anti-corruption.

13.14   The Definitive Glossary of Artificial Intelligence.

This glossary presents more than a thousand artificial intelligence concepts clearly explained, covering topics such as Machine Learning, Natural Language Processing, Computer Vision, and AI Ethics.

- Part 1 contemplates concepts starting with the letters A to D.
- Part 2 contemplates concepts initiated by the letters E to M.
- Part 3 contemplates concepts starting with the letters N to Z.

13.15   Prompt Engineering - Volumes 1 to 6.

This collection covers all the fundamentals of prompt engineering, providing a complete foundation for professional development.

With a rich variety of prompts for areas such as leadership, digital marketing, and information technology, it offers practical examples to improve clarity, decision-making, and gain valuable insights.

The volumes cover the following subjects:

- Volume 1: Fundamentals. Structuring Concepts and History of Prompt Engineering.
- Volume 2: Tools and Technologies, State and Context Management, and Ethics and Security.

- Volume 3: Language Models, Tokenization, and Training Methods.
- Volume 4: How to Ask Right Questions.
- Volume 5: Case Studies and Errors.
- Volume 6: The Best Prompts.

13.16   Guide to Being a Prompt Engineer – Volumes 1 and 2.

The collection explores the advanced fundamentals and skills required to be a successful prompt engineer, highlighting the benefits, risks, and the critical role this role plays in the development of artificial intelligence.

Volume 1 covers crafting effective prompts, while Volume 2 is a guide to understanding and applying the fundamentals of Prompt Engineering.

13.17   Data Governance with AI – Volumes 1 to 3.

Find out how to implement effective data governance with this comprehensive collection. Offering practical guidance, this collection covers everything from data architecture and organization to protection and quality assurance, providing a complete view to transform data into strategic assets.

Volume 1 addresses practices and regulations. Volume 2 explores in depth the processes, techniques, and best practices for conducting effective audits on data models. Volume 3 is your definitive guide to deploying data governance with AI.

13.18   Algorithm Governance.

This book looks at the impact of algorithms on society, exploring their foundations and addressing ethical and regulatory issues. It addresses transparency, accountability, and bias, with practical solutions for auditing and monitoring algorithms in sectors such as finance, health, and education.

13.19   From IT Professional to AI Expert: The Ultimate Guide to a Successful Career Transition.

For Information Technology professionals, the transition to AI represents a unique opportunity to enhance skills and contribute to the development of innovative solutions that shape the future.

In this book, we investigate the reasons for making this transition, the essential skills, the best learning path, and the prospects for the future of the IT job market.

13.20   Intelligent Leadership with AI: Transform Your Team and Drive Results.

This book reveals how artificial intelligence can revolutionize team management and maximize organizational performance.

By combining traditional leadership techniques with AI-powered insights, such as predictive analytics-based leadership, you'll learn how to optimize processes, make more strategic decisions, and create more efficient and engaged teams.

13.21   Impacts and Transformations: Complete Collection.

This collection offers a comprehensive and multifaceted analysis of the transformations brought about by Artificial Intelligence in contemporary society.

- Volume 1: Challenges and Solutions in the Detection of Texts Generated by Artificial Intelligence.

- Volume 2: The Age of Filter Bubbles. Artificial Intelligence and the Illusion of Freedom.
- Volume 3: Content Creation with AI - How to Do It?
- Volume 4: The Singularity Is Closer Than You Think.
- Volume 5: Human Stupidity versus Artificial Intelligence.
- Volume 6: The Age of Stupidity! A Cult of Stupidity?
- Volume 7: Autonomy in Motion: The Intelligent Vehicle Revolution.
- Volume 8: Poiesis and Creativity with AI.
- Volume 9: Perfect Duo: AI + Automation.
- Volume 10: Who Holds the Power of Data?

13.22   Big Data with AI: Complete Collection.

The collection covers everything from the technological fundamentals and architecture of Big Data to the administration and glossary of essential technical terms.

The collection also discusses the future of humanity's relationship with the enormous volume of data generated in the databases of training in Big Data structuring.

- Volume 1: Fundamentals.
- Volume 2: Architecture.
- Volume 3: Implementation.
- Volume 4: Administration.
- Volume 5: Essential Themes and Definitions.
- Volume 6: Data Warehouse, Big Data, and AI.

14 About the Author.

I'm Marcus Pinto, better known as Prof. Marcão, a specialist in information technology, information architecture and artificial intelligence.

With more than four decades of dedicated work and research, I have built a solid and recognized trajectory, always focused on making technical knowledge accessible and applicable to all those who seek to understand and stand out in this transformative field.

My experience spans strategic consulting, education and authorship, as well as an extensive performance as an information architecture analyst.

This experience enables me to offer innovative solutions adapted to the constantly evolving needs of the technological market, anticipating trends and creating bridges between technical knowledge and practical impact.

Over the years, I have developed comprehensive and in-depth expertise in data, artificial intelligence, and information governance – areas that have become essential for building robust and secure systems capable of handling the vast volume of data that shapes today's world.

My book collection, available on Amazon, reflects this expertise, addressing topics such as Data Governance, Big Data, and Artificial Intelligence with a clear focus on practical applications and strategic vision.

Author of more than 150 books, I investigate the impact of artificial intelligence in multiple spheres, exploring everything from its technical bases to the ethical issues that become increasingly urgent with the adoption of this technology on a large scale.

In my lectures and mentorships, I share not only the value of AI, but also the challenges and responsibilities that come with its implementation – elements that I consider essential for ethical and conscious adoption.

I believe that technological evolution is an inevitable path. My books are a proposed guide on this path, offering deep and accessible insights for those who want not only to understand, but to master the technologies of the future.

With a focus on education and human development, I invite you to join me on this transformative journey, exploring the possibilities and challenges that this digital age has in store for us.

15 How to Contact Prof. Marcão.

15.1 For lectures, training and business mentoring.

marcao.tecno@gmail.com

15.2 Prof. Marcão, on Linkedin.

https://bit.ly/linkedin_profmarcao